MANAGE
MY EMOTIONS
JOURNAL

What I Wish I'd Learned in School
About Anger, Fear, and Love

Kenneth J. Martz, Psy.D.

Copyright © 2020 by Kenneth Martz All rights reserved.

No part of this book may be reproduced in any form or by any means without the prior written permission of the publisher, excepting brief quotes used in connection with reviews, written specifically for inclusion in a magazine or newspaper.

Warning – Disclaimer: The purpose of this book is to educate. This book is not intended to take the place of professional counseling. It is a tool to support anyone in their personal journey of growth.

The author and/or publisher do not guarantee that anyone following these techniques, suggestions, tips, ideas, or strategies will become successful. The author and/or publisher shall have neither liability nor responsibility to anyone with respect to any loss or damage caused, or alleged to be caused, directly or indirectly, by the information contained in this book.

1st Printing Edition, December 2020

ISBN: 978-1-7357109-3-8 (Hardcover)

ISBN: 978-1-7357109-5-2 (Paperback)

ISBN: 978-1-7357109-4-5 (Digital)

www.DrKenMartz.com

WELCOME

When I wrote *Manage My Emotions*, I had no idea how popular it would become. My intent was simply to share insights, experiences, and tools to help others along their journey. After many requests and feedback for "more space" and other tools to support the journey, I developed this journal as a guide.

You are not required to read *Manage My Emotions* to benefit from this journal, although the text is aligned to this journal's topics and flow. Using both together can strengthen the benefit

Journaling is a powerful tool for self-discovery. In our busy lives, it helps to bring focus to our goals and success. It also brings relief to our struggles. It can help to calm our anxious, racing mind. It can help capture insights and much more.

Research on journaling has found dramatic effects such as reduced doctor's visits and improved immune function. As we develop emotional ease, there may be a link to reducing our *dis-ease*.

I designed this book as a tool to stimulate thinking, support your emotional management journey, and achieve success.

Writing engages a different part of the brain than reading. It has been found to significantly increase the likelihood of following through on our goals in life.

You may choose to use this journal in any way that works best for you. The content of this journal is generally aligned with the content of *Manage My Emotions*. Below are some suggestions:

- You may choose to use this as a traditional journal. Some of the questions and quotes may guide you or inspire you to a writing topic on a given day.
- You may write in your journal as notes when you are reading *Manage My Emotions*.
- You may decide to use a particular focus for your journal, such as starting each day with five things you are grateful for, five accomplishments, five things that were "fun" today, etc.
- You may want to use your journal to describe memories from the day or memories of troubling events from your past.
- Where possible, consider this to be your safe space to put any uncomfortable thoughts or feelings so that when you are finished, you can close the book and walk away.
- Another great use of journals is to write down goals for the next month, week, or day. Writing down our goals makes us much more likely to achieve them. (And checking them off can be quite satisfying.)
- Sometimes we are in a different emotional state with additional needs. Feel free to change up the way that you use your journal as needed.

Most importantly, this is your journal. Feel free to use it in any way that best serves you.

I have journaled for many years and found it incredibly helpful to capture ideas, maintain my motivation, and find clarity when I need it most. Hopefully, this tool will offer you the same as we continue this inward journey together.

Best wishes,

Kenneth J. Martz, Psy.D.

A NOTE TO MYSELF:

Why am I on this journey? What do I hope to learn or achieve?

DATE:

In addition to my initial "Why," are there a few other benefits I can get from this journey to help keep me motivated beyond my initial "Why"?

DATE:

_____
_____
_____
_____
_____
_____
_____
_____
_____
_____
_____
_____
_____
_____
_____
_____
_____
_____
_____

Kenneth J. Martz, Psy.D.

Let's start at the very beginning, a very good place to start...
- Julie Andrews

DATE:

_____

_____
_____
_____
_____
_____
_____
_____
_____
_____
_____
_____
_____
_____
_____
_____
_____
_____
_____

Where can I schedule 10 minutes into my day to read or journal regularly, every single day?

DATE:

How would I like my life to be like five years from now?

DATE:

With which emotions am I most comfortable? Uncomfortable?

DATE:

Is it possible for feelings to change? If so, how?

DATE:

_____

_____
_____
_____
_____
_____
_____
_____
_____
_____
_____
_____
_____
_____
_____
_____
_____
_____
_____

Am I deserving/worthy of a better emotional experience in life?

DATE:

Kenneth J. Martz, Psy.D.

The best and most beautiful things in the world cannot be seen or even touched - they must be felt with the heart.
- Helen Keller

DATE:

_____

_____
_____
_____
_____
_____
_____
_____
_____
_____
_____
_____
_____
_____
_____
_____
_____
_____
_____
_____
_____

How much of my day yesterday did I spend "blind" on autopilot?

DATE:

How can I increase awareness of my emotions?

DATE:

Which emotion am I feeling right now? Can I identify three emotions right now?

DATE:

_____

_____
_____
_____
_____
_____
_____
_____
_____
_____
_____
_____
_____
_____
_____
_____
_____
_____
_____

Which emotion am I feeling right now? If I didn't label the emotion, how long would it have continued on autopilot?

DATE:

What are my "go-to" escapes? Chocolate? Food? Screen time? Checking email/Facebook etc.?

DATE:

Who is one person that I blame for a problem? What is my own role/guilt in that problem?

DATE:

Manage My Emotions Journal

> *Always be true to your feelings, because the more you deny what you feel, the stronger it becomes.*
> — Anonymous

DATE:

_____

_____

_____

_____

_____

_____

_____

_____

_____

_____

_____

_____

_____

_____

_____

_____

_____

Can I think of a current challenge where I know I am "right"? Is there another emotion or honest perspective that I am denying?

DATE:

Manage My Emotions Journal

With which emotions do I not want to be associated? Fear? Anger?

DATE:

_____
_____
_____
_____
_____
_____
_____
_____
_____
_____
_____
_____
_____
_____
_____
_____
_____
_____

Kenneth J. Martz, Psy.D.

What happens when I pretend that I am not angry?

DATE:

Never make permanent decisions based on temporary feelings.
- Anonymous

DATE:

In order to feel "safe," how many "to do's" have I procrastinated or "repressed" in the past week?

DATE:

In the past week, what situations have I experienced "analysis paralysis," or have I been told that I am over thinking instead of acting?

DATE:

_____

_____
_____
_____
_____
_____
_____
_____
_____
_____
_____
_____
_____
_____
_____
_____
_____

Kenneth J. Martz, Psy.D.

*Somewhere between love and hate lies confusion,
misunderstanding and desperate hope.*
- Shannon L. Alder

DATE:

Just for today, how can I be honest with myself about my fears? Anger? Judgment?

DATE:

Which relationship do I keep score with someone, counting the ways that they "owe me"?

DATE:

Fear is a manipulative emotion that can trick us into living a boring life.
- Donald Miller

DATE:

_____

_____
_____
_____
_____
_____
_____
_____
_____
_____
_____
_____
_____
_____
_____
_____
_____
_____
_____

Choose one thing that scares me. How long have I held this fear?

DATE:

If you are carrying strong feelings about something that happened in your past. They may hinder your ability to live in the present.
- Les Brown

DATE:

Choosing one thing that I am afraid of, why have I held onto it for so long?

DATE:

Manage My Emotions Journal

In order to move on, you must understand why you felt what you did and why you no longer need to feel it.
- Mitch Albom

DATE:

_____
_____
_____
_____
_____
_____
_____
_____
_____
_____
_____
_____
_____
_____
_____
_____
_____
_____
_____
_____
_____
_____

If I misperceive an emotion (e.g., anger), so I am not aware of the hidden emotion (e.g., fear), how can I solve the "problem" rather than looking in the wrong place?

DATE:

Manage My Emotions Journal

I feel like I'm waiting for something that isn't going to happen.
- Anonymous

DATE:

Kenneth J. Martz, Psy.D.

How many feelings can I be aware of today?

DATE:

Choosing one of the moments of emotion that I have changed along the way, what new emotion emerged as the old emotion cleared?

DATE:

Is my motivation today different than when I started?

DATE:

Contentment and happiness depend solely on the mind, not on external objects or circumstances.
- Amma

DATE:

If my emotions mirror those around me, who is in my circle of friends, and what do they reflect back to me?

DATE:

If my emotions mirror things around me, what is reflected by my living space, email, TV channel, or other ways I spend my time?

DATE:

If I want to be happy, how can I surround myself with situations that will reflect that?

DATE:

If I google "happy news," what types of stories might be there today?

DATE:

If I have practiced an emotion (like sadness) for many days or weeks, it will become more and more familiar. Can I step outside of that emotion and observe this practice?

DATE:

Just for today, how can I practice happiness or pleasure for at least five minutes?

DATE:

We often think of trauma as an intensely emotional experience. Have there been times in my life that I have had sharp feedback and changed my behavior? (e.g., been hurt in a relationship and said, "I'll never do *that* again")

DATE:

_____
_____
_____
_____
_____
_____
_____
_____
_____
_____
_____
_____
_____
_____
_____
_____
_____
_____
_____

Identifying a recent hurt in my life, can I reframe it, choosing to see it differently? If so, perhaps I will do so?

DATE:

Choose a relationship where someone is regularly judging me, where I have come to expect them to judge me. If this individual brought me a gift today, would I accept it or expect some risk attached?

DATE:

Manage My Emotions Journal

Feelings are just visitors. Let them come and go.
- Mooji

DATE:

What emotion am I feeling right now? Repeat this question several times, writing down the answer. See how the answer change.

DATE:

Closing my eyes, I put my attention on my breath and observe my thoughts for one minute. How many thoughts occurred? How many emotions was I aware of? If there is that much change every minute, does this mean that it is possible for me to change?

DATE:

_____

_____
_____
_____
_____
_____
_____
_____
_____
_____
_____
_____
_____
_____
_____
_____

What emotion am I feeling right now? What sensations am I experiencing in my head, belly, head, or elsewhere that I label as that emotion? Is it possible that I could label that sensation as some other emotion?

DATE:

_____

_____

_____

_____

_____

_____

_____

_____

_____

_____

_____

_____

_____

_____

_____

_____

_____

As I look at the emotional circle (download at www.DrKenMartz.com), how many of the emotions am I experiencing today?

DATE:

As I look at the emotional, how many of the emotions am I NOT experiencing today? Recently? Is there a pattern?

DATE:

Manage My Emotions Journal

To be aware is to be alive.
- Anonymous

DATE:

_____
_____
_____
_____
_____
_____
_____
_____
_____
_____
_____
_____
_____
_____
_____
_____
_____
_____
_____
_____

If I am unaware of an emotion, how can I change it?

DATE:

Choosing something that I am afraid of, can I close my eyes and breathe for three minutes. How does the experience of fear change as I hold it with attention throughout several breaths?

DATE:

_____
_____
_____
_____
_____
_____
_____
_____
_____
_____
_____
_____
_____
_____
_____
_____
_____
_____
_____
_____
_____

Just for today, can I sit and observe my breath (meditate) for four minutes? How many things can I become aware of during this time?

DATE:

_____
_____
_____
_____
_____
_____
_____
_____
_____
_____
_____
_____
_____
_____
_____
_____
_____
_____

All emotions, even those that are suppressed and unexpressed, have physical effects. Unexpressed emotions tend to stay in the body like small ticking time bombs —they are illnesses in incubation.
- Marilyn Van M. Derbur

DATE:

Chose a situation that is causing me to experience an emotion. Ask myself, is it true? Am I absolutely sure that my perception is accurate?

DATE:

Identify one emotion that I am experiencing today. Can I recognize my associated physical sensations, beliefs, imagery, and cultural influence of this emotion?

DATE:

Identify one emotion that I am experiencing today. Consider how this experience would change if I were of a different gender, race, religion, nationality, or cultural identity.

DATE:

Manage My Emotions Journal

Talent is a pursued interest. Anything that you're willing to practice, you can do.
- Bob Ross

DATE:

Just for today, I can practice smiling. Setting a timer, I can smile or laugh once an hour. Smiling will benefit me and all those around me.

DATE:

Just for today, I will, for the sake of my loved one, practice gratitude by writing down at bedtime at least four things I am grateful for. I will remind myself by placing the journal next to my bed so I can remember to write it down. This practice will help me and all those around me, and I will check in by reviewing it in my journal tomorrow.

DATE:

What was the experience of identifying gratitude like? Was it easy or difficult? How did I feel differently afterward? Is this something I might want to continue for more than one day?

DATE:

We each reflect the same sun. The sun shines down, and its image reflects in a thousand different pots filled with water. The reflections are many, but they are each reflecting the same sun. Similarly, when we come to know who we truly are, we will see ourselves in all people.
- Amma

DATE:

Just for today, or planning for tomorrow, can I take one task from idea, through development, completion, and enjoy the success before letting go to make room for the next task? I probably do this many times every day.

DATE:

Manage My Emotions Journal

Fear is the path to the Dark Side. Fear leads to anger. Anger leads to hate. Hate leads to suffering.
       - Yoda

DATE:

What is one thing that scares me? When is the first time I recall having this fear?

DATE:

Manage My Emotions Journal

Never take someone's feelings for granted because you never know how much courage that they took to show it to you.
- Anonymous

DATE:

If I didn't have this fear, how would my life be different today?

DATE:

What are some things that my fear has stopped me from doing? Has this protected me, or would I like to strengthen the courage to complete these things?

DATE:

I am stronger than I think. What can I do today to help me remember this?

DATE:

For just five minutes, can I imagine myself as strong and full of courage? Notice how the experience changes at about three minutes.

DATE:

Kenneth J. Martz, Psy.D.

Don't hide your feelings. Act on them. You never know when that chance will no longer be there.
- Anonymous

DATE:

What is one thing that makes me feel angry or annoyed? Is there a fear or risk that I face, hidden underneath the anger?

DATE:

_____

_____
_____
_____
_____
_____
_____
_____
_____
_____
_____
_____
_____
_____
_____
_____
_____
_____
_____
_____

What is my vision for myself in 5 years? How would I like to be? What is one small thing I can do today toward that goal?

DATE:

Manage My Emotions Journal

Anger is the feeling that makes your mouth work faster than your mind.
- Anonymous

DATE:

What is my vision for myself in 1 year? How would I like to be? What is one small thing I can do today toward that goal?

DATE:

What is one emotion I would like to experience in the next three months? What is one small thing I can do today toward that goal?

DATE:

Kenneth J. Martz, Psy.D.

Let anyone who comes to you go away feeling better and happier. Everyone should see goodness in your face, in your eyes, in your smile. Joy shows from the eyes. It appears when we speak and walk. It cannot be kept closed inside us. It reacts outside. Joy is very infectious.
- Mother Teresa

DATE:

Who can I smile at today? Can I smile at them and mentally share with them the warm center of my heart?

DATE:

Are the joys in my life being overshadowed by grief or fear?

DATE:

What are three things I can do today to play?

DATE:

Smile now. Notice the lightness that comes with the sensations. If it feels good, decide how long to hold before letting it go. I can repeat it often.

DATE:

Research has shown that a simple act of kindness directed toward another improves the functioning of the immune system and stimulates the production of serotonin in both the recipient of the kindness and the person extending the kindness. Kindness extended, received, or observed beneficially impacts the physical health and feelings of everyone involved.
- Wayne Dyer

DATE:

What random act of kindness can I offer today?

DATE:

What gift can offer to take care of someone today (e.g., holding the door for them, wiping a tear, easing their load)

DATE:

Just for today, how many tastes can I savor? Whatever food I eat today, can I sit and enjoy it?

DATE:

If I choose to bless another person, I will always end up feeling more blessed.
- Marianne Williamson

DATE:

What can I clean today? Take 20 minutes to clean your inbox, clear your "junk-drawer," throw out some unneeded items, etc.

DATE:

What is one anger that I can forgive today? Is it possible to be at peace for one minute? Let it go and notice the difference. Forgiveness is about easing our own pain, not the other's pain.

DATE:

Kenneth J. Martz, Psy.D.

If you are carrying strong feelings about something that happened in your past. They may hinder your ability to live in the present.
- Les Brown

DATE:

_____
_____
_____
_____
_____
_____
_____
_____
_____
_____
_____
_____
_____
_____
_____
_____
_____
_____
_____

Is this loss the end of the story or the end of a chapter?

DATE:

Are losses in my life the endings or lessons learned for my next movement through the next chapter of life?

DATE:

Manage My Emotions Journal

When we think that God is with us, all our burdens will be lessened. Once we have entered a boat or bus, why should we continue to carry the luggage? Put it down.
- Amma

DATE:

What do I hold as valuable, more precious than gold?

DATE:

What can I do today to touch the sacred in life? Pray? Be honest? Feel respect for my beloved?

DATE:

Kenneth J. Martz, Psy.D.

A human being is a part of the whole called by us universe, a part limited in time and space. He experiences himself, his thoughts and feelings as something separated from the rest, a kind of optical delusion of his consciousness. This delusion is a kind of prison for us, restricting us to our personal desires and to affection for a few persons nearest to us. Our task must be to free ourselves from this prison by widening our circle of compassion to embrace all living creatures and the whole of nature in its beauty.
- Albert Einstein

DATE:

Manage My Emotions Journal

Who do I love? Do I share with them my full range of emotions?

DATE:

Are there places I get "stuck," experiencing certain emotions but not others? Which ones are easier or more challenging for me?

DATE:

Attitude is a choice. Happiness is a choice. Optimism is a choice. Kindness is a choice. Giving is a choice. Respect is a choice. Whatever choice you make makes you. Choose wisely.
- Roy T. Bennett

DATE:

Am I motivated more to escape problems or toward my goals?

DATE:

Don't be pushed around by the fears in your mind.
Be led by the dreams in your heart.
- Roy T. Bennett

DATE:

Do I have a compelling vision of my goals?

DATE:

Where did I develop my beliefs about motivation?

DATE:

You can talk with someone for years, every day, and still, it won't mean as much as what you can have when you sit in front of someone, not saying a word, yet you feel that person with your heart, you feel like you have known the person forever... connections are made with the heart, not the tongue.
- C. JoyBell C.

DATE:

Do habitually practice passivity, assertiveness, or aggressiveness?

DATE:

What fears or feelings of not being worthy get in the way of my assertiveness?

DATE:

Are there situations where I am better able to be emotionally neutral and assertive?

DATE:

Just for today, how can I be clear about one thing that I want and make an assertive request for it?

DATE:

*Love is a combination of admiration, respect, and passion.
If you have one of those going, that's par for the course.
If you have two, you aren't quite world-class, but you're close.
If you have all three, then you don't need to die;
You're already in Heaven.*
- William Wharton

DATE:

How can I deepen the trust of the relationship with my beloved today?

DATE:

Manage My Emotions Journal

What can I give to my beloved today?

DATE:

What can I do today to surprise my beloved, showing them how I appreciate something they have done?

DATE:

Manage My Emotions Journal

> *The best feeling in the world is…*
> *When you look at that special person and*
> *they are already smiling at you.*
> - Anonymous

DATE:

Just for today, can I allow my beloved to support me?

DATE:

Just for today, what task can I accomplish together with my partner?

DATE:

Is there something I could practice daily that only takes seconds to build a better relationship over time?

DATE:

Manage My Emotions Journal

> *The culture of a workplace - an organization's values, norms, and practices - has a huge impact on our happiness and success.*
> - Adam Grant

DATE:

What can I do or achieve to offer more value to the organization today?

DATE:

_____
_____
_____
_____
_____
_____
_____
_____
_____
_____
_____
_____
_____
_____
_____
_____
_____
_____
_____
_____

Is there any "wasted time" today that I could turn into productivity?

DATE:

___

Just for today, what is one thing I can do or say to build more team and community in my workplace?

DATE:

Manage My Emotions Journal

*Our greatest glory is not in never falling,
but in getting up every time we do.*
- Confucius

DATE:

What habits do I have that regularly limit my full potential?

DATE:

What situations cause me to emotionally react, escaping into chemicals or behaviors that don't serve me long term?

DATE:

What step can I take today to move toward a different pattern of responding?

DATE:

What supports from outside of myself are needed to be successful with the fastest and most effective results?

DATE:

Kenneth J. Martz, Psy.D.

A nation's culture resides in the hearts and in the soul of its people.
- Mahatma Gandhi

DATE:

Manage My Emotions Journal

How does my gender affect my handling of fear and anger?

DATE:

If I was a different race, how would my experience at my job site be different?

DATE:

How have my family's expectations supported or limited my career and long-term goals?

DATE:

Kenneth J. Martz, Psy.D.

The task is not so much to see what no one has yet seen, but to think what nobody has yet thought, about that which everybody sees.
- Erwin Schrödinger

DATE:

Choose a challenge in my life. Is there another perspective or approach that might be more effective?

DATE:

There are hundreds of tools. Which one new tool can I try today?

DATE:

Watch your thoughts. They become words;
Watch your words. They become actions;
Watch your actions. They become habits;
Watch your habits. They become character;
Watch your character, for it becomes your destiny.
-Frank Outlaw

DATE:

_____

_____
_____
_____
_____
_____
_____
_____
_____
_____
_____
_____
_____
_____
_____
_____
_____

Using my values, how can I choose and practice a tool or tools until I become an expert?

DATE:

Politics is a profession; a serious, complicated and, in its true sense, a noble one.
- Dwight D. Eisenhower

DATE:

Just as my family has expectations, my local, state, and country have rules and laws. How can I act in alignment with these practices?

DATE:

Just as my family has expectations, my local, state, and country have rules and laws. What can I do today to move toward changing one of these rules that do not serve the community?

DATE:

We have two eyes but one vision.
- Amma

DATE:

Just for today, can I see something from someone else's perspective?

DATE:

Kenneth J. Martz, Psy.D.

You can't start the next chapter in your life if you are still reading the last one.
- Anonymous

DATE:

What is the most important thing I have learned on this journey?

DATE:

What are my next steps to build on what I have learned?

DATE:

What else can I put in place to practice these skills for a lifetime?

DATE:

ABOUT THE AUTHOR

Kenneth J. Martz, Psy.D. is a licensed psychologist working in treating and managing mental health and addiction for the past twenty-five years. He has specialty training in Chinese medicine, yoga, meditation, and hypnosis. He is also skilled in a range of supervision and management techniques.

Dr. Martz has authored over a dozen publications and has served on eight completed doctoral dissertation committees. He has offered over 100 local, national, and international presentations in the mental health and addiction treatment field. You can find earlier works on Amazon in *The Downside: Problem and Pathological Gambling* and in *A Public Health Guide to Ending the Opioid Epidemic*.

If you enjoyed this book, please take a moment to help someone else by sharing a brief review and follow me at your favorite bookseller websites.

Feel free to continue your journey with me from my website, where you will find new resources, tools, and advance notice of new books at www.DrKenMartz.com

Free Gifts!

Be sure to check out my website at www.DrKenMartz.com for updates on free material, seminars, forthcoming books, and more.

Be sure to download a range of free tools to support your journey, such as the Emotion Circle, How to Meditate, Relaxation Techniques and the Manage My Emotions Checklist.

Kenneth J. Martz, Psy.D.

See also Manage My Emotions

In this valuable self-improvement guide for managing emotions, you will learn:

- What emotions really are, how they become ingrained into your daily life
- Amazingly effective self-assessment exercises
- 8 powerful ways to conquer fear
- 14 thoughtful tools to manage anger
- 12 easy exercises to quiet our worry
- To find the motivation to succeed, passion for life, and learn to cherish positive relationships with spouses, your children, and your friends

What Are They Saying about Manage My Emotions?
- "A highly recommended read" **5 Star Rating** *Tammy Wong*
- "Take back control and live our lives to the fullest." **5 Star Rating** *Rabia Tanveer*
- "Exactly the book I needed…and I believe it will resonate with many other readers." **5 Star Rating** *Jamie Michele*
- "Manage your emotions and learn to live well!" *Dr. Sandra Rasmussen*
- "Will help a lot of people" *Penny Fletcher*
- "An outstanding job of offering solutions" *Joel Elston*

Continue your journey. Get your copy today.

COMING SOON

Manage My Emotions *for Kids*

The Manage My Emotions journey is based on the idea that I wish I had learned these things sooner. Many readers have also echoed this concern. If you have enjoyed this material, you can soon share this with your children.

Manage My Emotions for Kids is aligned with the exercises in this text. It will help you to:

- Reinforce your learning of these concepts
- Teach your children these lessons early
- Set your children on the right track
- Open meaningful conversations and communication.

Manage My Addiction

An estimated 24 million Americans are in recovery from Substance Use Disorder. Many more experience active substance use, as well as other addictive processes such as gambling, eating, spending, and screentime.

Manage My Addiction expands on the Manage My Emotions journey with new tools and insights to guide lasting changes.

Kenneth J. Martz, Psy.D.

www.ingramcontent.com/pod-product-compliance
Lightning Source LLC
Chambersburg PA
CBHW071856160426
43209CB00005B/1075